CHARLES R. **STINSON** ARCHITECTS

To the foundation of my life—
My wife Carol, children Jason, Joshua and Jessica,
and daughter-in-law Shawna,
grandchildren Landon, Tennison, Wilder and inspirations yet to come,
parents, Robert and Harriette,
sisters Ann and Karen,
and father-in-law Alfred—
you have made the dream beautiful and complete.

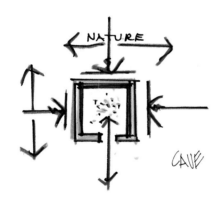

CAVE

COMPOSITION

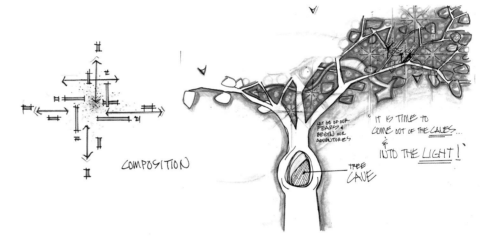

LET GO OF OUR
FEARS &
BEGIN OUR
ADVENTURES

"IT IS TIME TO
COME OUT OF THE CAVES...
&
INTO THE _LIGHT_!"

TREE
CAVE

Wright and Biederman's work. "In architecture school, we learned a methodology focused on arranging boxes, then scooping out holes in those boxes to move from room to room," Stinson explains. "It was about being in the trunk of the tree and carving holes out. Wright and Biederman were about living in the spaces between the branches and leaves." From that moment on, Stinson's architecture evolved into a signature style of vertical, horizontal, and sometimes curved forms artfully juxtaposed to maximize the house's response to site, vegetation, and sun. He also uses these forms, whose function may change as they extend from the exterior of the house through to the interior, to shape spaces of ever-changing light and warmth.

One of Stinson's clients offered these insights about his body of work: "The sleek lines of Charles' houses are reminiscent of the Prairie School style with their horizontal planes and

vertical cuts. But the point of his architecture is energy; the communication of one form with another in a celebration of how energy flows." Such word choices as energy and flow, in addition to descriptors like "organic process" and "harmonic connection," are also used by Stinson to describe his creative process.

After he has met with a client to discuss their functional needs, lifestyle requirements, and visions for a new home, Stinson begins his creative process by walking the site. He absorbs the slope and vegetation, records the patterns of sun and shade throughout the day, and decides which views to maximize or minimize. He then imagines "the design concept floating on the site," and brings in "the simple, individual forms—the thinner the better, and one at a time—to define uplifting, inspiring living spaces."

"Each horizontal, vertical, curved, or sloping form has to serve any number of needs—hold up a roof, carry electricity, block a street, or focus a view—while compositionally corresponding with the other forms," Stinson continues. As he moves "indoors" on the site, imagining the concept from the inside out, the exterior and interior coalesce into "a living entity whose composition condenses and releases energy," he says. In other words, through the careful placement of each form, Stinson simultaneously creates a sanctuary in one space, in another an expansive connection with the outdoors, and in others such details as built-in window seats or a child's fort beneath a stairwell.

Stinson's design philosophy and the convictions underpinning it are inseparable from his accessibility and warmth, his Zen-like approach to challenge, his perennial optimism, and his genuine delight in every project. His favorite adages include, "Each client is and shall remain a friend" and "We've never given up on a project or a client." His calling card, however, is the architecture, which in turn attracts a particular kind of person.

"Almost all of our clients are self-made or entrepreneurs or creative professionals," Stinson says. "They're strong-willed and strong-minded people. They come to us because of a harmonic connection they feel with the architecture they've

already experienced, whether they've seen one of our projects in a book or magazine, or walked through one of our houses." Because the finished house must support and enhance the clients' current and future lives, Stinson's designs evolve as clients respond to changes and developments. "We don't finalize a solution unless everyone agrees," he says. "If someone blinks, we know it won't work. If everyone's eyes sparkle, we've succeeded. The entire team—from our office and our clients, to the builders and subcontractors—has to believe in this process. One of my jobs is to create an atmosphere of trust among everyone."

In 2001, Stinson expanded this aesthetic and practical approach toward the single project into the broader realms of land planning and development. With his long-time Minnesota collaborators, builders Streeter & Associates, and landscape architects Coen + Partners, Stinson innovated two new architectural communities.

On pristine wooded acreage next to Lotus Lake in Chanhassen, the site of a former children's summer camp, Stinson designed a nearly road-less development that preserves the area's mature maple and oak trees. Each home, designed with the buyer, features Stinson's signature forms composed to foster an uplifting relationship between structure and site, between indoor living and access to the outdoors. Stinson intends the ensemble of houses near Lotus Lake to eventually combine into one dynamic architectural composition. Similarly, Stinson's Biltmore development, which he planned on a wooded city parcel adjacent to urban parkland on Cedar Lake in Minneapolis, also features individual houses sensitively sited and designed so when the development is completed, each will relate to the larger whole. As Stinson's practice moves well in the 21st century, he has found "that green technology is catching up with the architectural possibilities." Since he began practicing, Stinson has always incorporated within his compositional strategies such principles of good architecture as operable windows situated for cross-ventilation, and forms aligned to maximize or minimize sun according to the seasons.

8

However, the advent of such new technologies as geothermal heating, photovoltaic cells, and high-performance windows and mechanicals, as well as recycled materials and reclaimed woods, has opened up new possibilities for a green aesthetic in architecture that's distinctly Stinson's own. "These new materials and technologies are easily integrated into the compositional language of proportion and harmonics I've developed," he says.

At the same time, prior aesthetic, technological, and material distinctions between his practice's commercial and residential work are becoming delightfully blurred. "We're mixing things up to develop new hybrids," he explains, "by bringing commercial construction materials like steel and concrete, and technologies like geothermal heating into our residential projects. Conversely, we're bringing residential scales of intimacy into our commercial projects."

Stinson has also begun applying his compositional strategies, now embedded with green technologies, to the renovation of existing structures, most notably a 100-year-old farmhouse in a new section of the Lotus Lake development. "Right now we're excited about developing and applying our new green architectural language to the renovation of older houses," he says.

For more than 30 years, Stinson has honed an original compositional methodology elastic enough to encompass a range of site conditions and geographical locations, and project types from a bank to a poolside gazebo, an entire master-planned community to a condominium, a new lakeside or urban home to a rural renovation. With his most recent project, a new home near Lake Calhoun in Minneapolis, Stinson feels he's reaching a new milestone in his architectural career.

Designed for clients "who wanted something completely new," Stinson says, the concrete-and-steel structure, clad in local limestone, will be heated by passive solar through triple-glazed windows, as well as with photovoltaic cells and geothermal wells. The house features a green roof with deck, turf, and gardens, reached by a stair tower constructed of commercial glass. The interior will be clad in wood from trees harvested and sold by Wisconsin co-operatives. "The detailing," he adds, "challenged us to come up with solutions we've never used before."

"In many ways," Stinson continues, "this project brings us to the end of a chapter and the beginning of another. We feel we're stepping into a whole new world of architectural design and client relationships." He continues to adhere to an architectural philosophy centered on composing buildings, collaborations, and relationships "in which everyone wins," he adds, "which is also the philosophy of my life."

But as his practice moves forward alongside advances in green technologies and materials, and with national and international clients whose visions of an architectural future surpass even his own, Stinson's self-appointed challenge is to evolve his singular architectural methodology to encompass, with integrity and flexibility, new possibilities as they reveal themselves.

For anyone who enters that trajectory, Stinson remains the creative force that holds each project together. "Architecture is about the invisible, like faith," he says. "It's about manifesting the dreams people have." As Stinson's practice and design philosophies evolve, he's ready to travel the world, sketchbook and colored pencils in hand, to make that happen.

PROJECTS

It is my deepest desire to inspire. It is my hope that the joy of creation will radiate in other lives, bringing closer mankind's natural state of peace and harmony.

— Charles R. Stinson

STINSON/EASTLUND RESIDENCE
Deephaven, Minnesota

An Urban Cabin for Open Living

In 1993, Charles Stinson applied his compositional theories of light, line, and plane in the design of his family's 2,700-square-foot, four-bedroom home. A framework of white verticals and horizontals, accented by a thin blue line along the fascia, supports glass expanses topped with clerestory windows, creating an open interior in which light, sightlines, and energy flow unimpeded. Corner window seats offer panoramic views of the backyard, while wide decks offer opportunities for outdoor living.

In 2005, Stinson and his wife Carol Eastlund decided expand those outdoor living options and tame the "wild tangle" in their backyard. Several tons of fill provided the foundation for a salt-water pool surrounded by white stucco walls. Thin metal railings, which echo the rails of the house's upper deck and its rooflines, top the walls. Around the pool, bands of custom-cut Fond du Lac limestone also reflect the lines of the house.

Stinson designed the cabana with his signature vertical "fins" and a roof of clear-cedar slats. The underside of the house, where three glass-walled bedrooms open out onto the pool area, is also clad in clear cedar. A new spiral staircase connects the expanded outdoor-living space with the house's upper deck. More than 50 mature trees were planted to create woodland behind the pool area.

On summer mornings, Charles and Carol walk out of their bedroom and enjoy coffee by the pool. The couple's three adult children—Jason, Joshua and Jess—bring their families and friends over for poolside parties. The family's backyard is now a Zen sanctuary for summer enjoyment.

The front of the house maintains a low, open profile with a spacious auto court available for car parking, ping-pong games or tricycle races, while the back of the residence, enclosed by trees and lawn, rises horizontally from the new cabana and pool.

14

The open, light-filled living area, outlined by a continuous band of clerestory windows, flows into more secluded spaces beneath lowered ceilings.

From the kitchen, views to the sky, the front entrance and the backyard are ever-present via strategically placed windows and openings.

18 The backyard before the addition of the saltwater pool and cabana (opposite), and after (below). The lower-level bedrooms now open directly onto the addition, which is seamlessly connected to the house through the use of repeating horizontal and vertical elements, and the use of clear-cedar siding as the cabana canopy and along the underside of the house's outdoor ceiling.

PRIVATE RESIDENCE
Rolling Green, Minnesota

22

A guest arrival area, and low broad limestone steps, lead to the formal entry of this 7,000-square-foot home, one of Stinson's first major commissions.

The spacious living area is punctuated with square clerestory windows (above, opposite top), which continue in the casual eating area off the kitchen with corner booth (opposite).

A dramatic curved stairway threads the house's three levels together (above), and overlooks the formal dining area with its window wall and views to the gardens (opposite).

The 3,000-square-foot house is tucked into its wedge-shaped site on a cul-de-sac near a lake (opposite), with the main living level located above the tuck-under garage and accessed through a landscaped terrace (above).

Designed for a couple, the house has a formal, open-living plan (opposite top), and features clerestory windows that crown the dining area with sunlight and starlight (opposite bottom). An efficient galley kitchen includes a playful combination of light cherry wood on the upper cabinets and dark cherry on the lower cabinets (above).

BURT RESIDENCE
North Shore
Lake Superior, Minnesota

Spread across a wooded site next to Lake Superior, the house's low limestone profile grounds a rippling roof that mimics waves cresting on the lake.

BEALEAU RESIDENCE
Lake Crystal, Minnesota

34

The exterior was rigorously composed of white vertical and horizontal planes, the latter outlined in blue fascia that connects the home to the lake and the sky.

With its broad thin steps and entry plane, the house seemingly floats on its site (above), as do second-floor windows that cantilever slightly to absorb exterior views and provide space for window seats inside (opposite).

PRIVATE RESIDENCE
Lake Minnetonka, Minnesota

The 4,000-square-foot home is a simple composition of broad horizontals framing glass expanses subtly anchored with thin verticals (above), which continues inside as a frame for a light-filled, open interior in which one side of the fireplace holds built-in shelving for artwork (opposite).

40 The other side the fireplace anchors a sitting area alongside a wall of windows that open to the upper deck overlooking the lake (above). The low inviting entry steps into the open living area lit by clerestory windows and warmed with Brazilian cherry floors (below). Perched over the lake, the house includes three bedrooms that walk out to the lawn and lake on the lower level (opposite).

BUUCK RESIDENCE
Bloomington, Minnesota

The low, rough-shingled roof and variegated, Chilton-limestone walls of this home create a rustic aesthetic (above) that is smoothed into clean, contemporary lines and forms inside, where skylights, picture windows and window ribbons insert natural light (opposite).

SANDERS RESIDENCE
Cottagewood
Deephaven, Minnesota

The five-level home—with main living area located on the top floor to maximize views—steps down its steep slope to the pond and features two decks for wildlife watching.

FLEMING RESIDENCE
Minnetonka, Minnesota

With a quiet nod to the Prairie School of architecture, the clean lines of the exterior were accomplished with a knife-edge roof free of fascia, thin vertical forms that rise up through a roof opening alongside a birch tree, and a low sheltered entry that opens into a high-ceilinged great room.

In the open plan great room, dropped soffits subtly divide the sitting area from the dining room (opposite), while the fireplace warms the entire living area on one side and defines the stairway to the lower-level media room, office, and bedrooms on the other (above).

In the 5,000-square-foot, two-level home, a vaulted ceiling augments the living area's spacious feeling (opposite), while the lower ceiling over the kitchen provides a homey intimacy next to the family room with windows to the outdoors (above).

Sited on an infill lot, the four-bedroom house includes windows to the adjacent woods, providing a panorama of green in the formal sitting area/piano room (above).

CHARLES R. STINSON ARCHITECTS & CRS INTERIORS OFFICE AND STUDIO

Deephaven, Minnesota

Stinson's office building showcases the architect's compositional style with its simple
juxtaposition of horizontal and vertical forms.

Clerestory windows top broad window expanses, while vertical forms define the office's welcome area and conference room with their clean color palette of warm yellow, fresh white, and Aegean blue.

WILSON RESIDENCE
Bear Path
Eden Prairie, Minnesota

The three-level home, located in a gated, golf-course community, features a rustic combination of limestone forms below a cedar-shake roof.

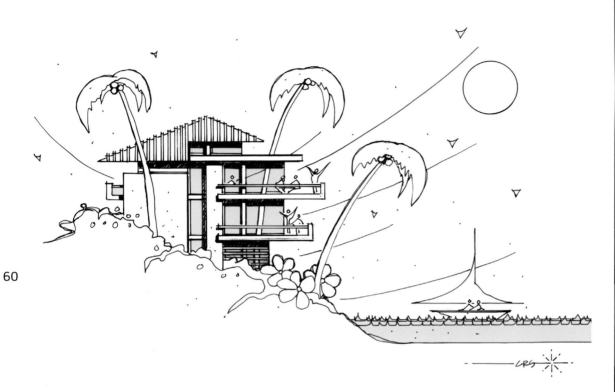

60

Located on an inter-coastal waterway, this two-unit structure provides vacation
condominiums with wrap-around decks overlooking the busy thoroughfare (opposite).
Inside the third-level penthouse, clerestory windows bring high light deep into the
open-plan unit for sunlit casual living (above).

The structure was sited on a peninsula next to mangroves (top, above), and includes plenty of outdoor living opportunities, from extended balconies to a rooftop terrace and garden with views to the Gulf of Mexico (opposite).

CORSON RESIDENCE
Lake Minnetonka, Minnesota

Home Within a House

This dual-function residence on the shore of Lake Minnetonka was designed for a couple who had specific goals in mind. Both husband and wife are executives and philanthropists who desired an architectural showcase in which to entertain up to 50 of their friends and colleagues during fundraisers. They also wanted a private retreat embedded within the 7,000-square-foot house: intimate, elegant, and packed with amenities.

The drama begins at the canopied front entrance, and moves inside to the foyer where eight windows from Frank Lloyd Wright's dismantled Little House (which originally was sited adjacent to this home) hang inside the windows. The foyer then opens into a glass-walled reception room that seemingly floats over the lower level and opens to a grand deck that cantilevers out toward the lake.

Floor-to-ceiling windows crowned with transom windows and a scale-reducing, 9-foot soffit, along with a skylight above the room's center table, usher in plentiful light. At night, when lit from within, the room casts a welcoming glow. After cocktail hour, guests descend to the house's lower level for sit-down dining (this space also doubles as the family room). Glass doors open to a deck and a catering kitchen allows for food preparation.

Nestled within Stinson's striking composition of horizontal and vertical forms, just off the reception room, is the couple's private wing. Here an open kitchen/family room/sunroom is closely related to the couple's bedroom and her office alcove. The lakeside retreat also includes built-in window seats, a fireplace, glass-inset doors to the deck, and a skylight over the eating area, all of which add charm to the home-within-a-house's fresh aesthetic.

Arts and Crafts-style window banding illuminates the house's formal entrance, with glass doors opening to views through the house and the lake beyond.

The front entry of the 7,000-square-foot house opens to the formal dining area with Prairie-style windows overlooking the lake and French doors opening onto the terrace (above). Stairwells lead to the informal living areas below, which also overlook the lake through walls of windows (opposite).

From the front entry, the homeowners walk to the lower level (opposite) with its spacious informal living area (right) and bedrooms with views to the outdoors (below).

The house was composed to reach out toward the lake (above), with broad rooflines that shelter outdoor balconies on the upper floors and recede on lower balconies (opposite).

Even when rainswept, the house's vertical limestone and stucco forms anchor the upper terrace and cantilevered balcony (opposite), which seems to float into the treetops toward the lake (above).

74

Brick forms from the house's exterior continue inside to add texture to the sleek horizontals and light walls designed to provide space and shelving for the homeowners' artwork and art objects. A curved stairwell and railing also soften the angular planes of the space (opposite).

The great room in the 4,000-square-foot house is essentially one long form with window walls on each end (below), one of which overlooks the home's floating entrance canopy (opposite bottom). A see-through fireplace connects, and yet defines, the formal and informal seating areas of the house, as do soffits and ceilings raised to varying heights (opposite top).

ALTMAN RESIDENCE
Minnetonka, Minnesota

Flight of Imagination

In the early 1990s, Frank and Leslie Altman purchased a lot on a peninsula overlooking ponds and wetlands, and decided to build new. The couple asked Stinson to design a house that would fly or float on the natural site. They also encouraged the architect to free his imagination and design a structure that was both innovative and organic.

Stinson nestled one end of the two-level, four-bedroom house into an adjacent hill; on the opposite end, he composed a triangular atrium and balcony that surges out into the wooded landscape like a ship's prow. Behind the atrium the 4,500-square-foot house's living spaces extend as wings from a central spine. From the outside, the house's geometry of forms—painted dark blue, forest green, terracotta, and yellow—appear to float along the natural site like a butterfly coming to rest.

Inside, color also defines the house's open living spaces, as do the circular soffits that lower the ceiling heights to a more intimate scale. Expansive views to the outdoors can be enjoyed from almost any location on the main living level, while ceilings were pitched and walls configured in private areas—such as the master bedroom—to allow light to penetrate the rooms.

In the lower-level bedrooms, Stinson designed elevated areas with built-in cabinets, and desks for work or study. A "fort" hidden beneath the stairs provides a hideaway for children. Geometry, form, color, and texture combine in a composition of organic complexity in the Altman Residence, which perches weightlessly on its elevated site with wings outstretched.

The house rises up and opens out from its narrow base like a ship afloat in its wooded setting.

An ensemble of blue peaked and horizontal forms, stabilized by strong red verticals, the house is an artful composition of broad grounded spaces and roof lines appearing to take flight, repeated throughout the house's interiors.

Inside, the interiors are softened by curved space-defining
shapes in the soffited ceilings, on the floor, in the furnishings,
and as part of the stairwell.

Curved soffited ceilings extend from the living area (opposite above) into the bedroom, bringing in daylight and architectural forms that define the sleeping area (opposite below). Lower ceilings in the sitting area near the kitchen give the room a more enclosed, cozy ambience (below).

The blue rooflines and red pillars blend in with the autumn
foliage of the wooded, lakeside site (below), while the house's
prow rises up amid the trees around it.

NORDAHL RESIDENCE
Bloomington, Minnesota

The Asian-inspired exterior of the 5,500-square-foot house on a
wooded hilltop features cream stucco walls with large window
expanses framed in black beneath large roof overhangs, some
which protect decks and balconies extending into the site.

Inside the sunlit house a minimalist interior is warmed with maple cabinetry and floors (right), while soffits and pitched ceilings define living areas (opposite). In the kitchen, placed in a corner for optimal views, clean-lined cabinets float on the walls, separated by windows that maximize natural light and provide connections with the outdoors (below).

COLE RESIDENCE
Mississippi River Bluff
Prescott, Wisconsin

Because the homeowners wanted panoramic views of the scenic river from the bluff-top site, the limestone-and-stucco home was composed as a series of forms at 60-degree angles, topped with strikingly angular, projected-gable roofs.

The geometry continues inside the 4,500-square-foot house, as the kitchen is nestled into a corner with angled cabinetry (opposite top). Angled limestone columns and zig-zagging soffits also echo the house's dramatic angles, while floors of pecan and hickory wood, and cedar-clad ceilings create a warmth and intimacy that contrasts with the panoramic river views (opposite bottom, above).

PRIVATE RESIDENCE
Olympic Hills Golf Course, Minnesota

The exterior of this 3,700-square-foot summer home for a retired couple is a tightly layered composition of thin horizontal planes, accentuated by double clerestories, the window box, and a garden portico.

Pine-framed clerestories bring sunlight into the first level of the two-story walkout, which features a long open plan for informal family gatherings (above). The double clerestories over the staircase create a lightwell that draws sun to the lower level (right, opposite).

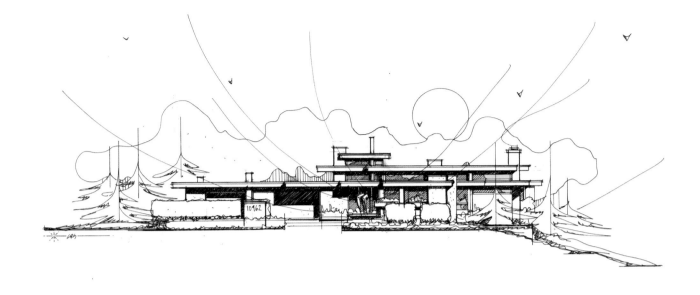

LEESA AND SAM'S HOUSE
Christmas Lake, Excelsior, Minnesota

Playful and Sophisticated Simplicity

Leesa Nahki-Brown had a dream: to build an uplifting home in which she and her son could live comfortably, and with a media room in which Sam could hang out privately with his friends. Stinson began by composing a 3,200-square-foot, two-bedroom house that derives much of its playful spirit from simple, sophisticated planes in primary colors juxtaposed with those painted white.

He also designed two-story windows in a squared-off U shape, which give the house tremendous transparency. From the outside, visitors can see straight through the white-stucco house to nearby Christmas Lake. From the inside, the notion of interior and exterior is virtually erased. As a result, the house rests on its site awash in light, with strategically placed roof overhangs shielding the interior from direct sun in the summer.

The U-shape continues inside the great room, where the square fireplace, framed in glass block and red-painted forms, features an inverted-U cutout supporting a glass shelf wrapped in maple. Through pocket doors to the right is Sam's media room with a pool table and large-screen television.

Opposite the great room, square-U shelving intersects a glass plane in the built-in buffet that separates the dining area and kitchen. White Corian wraps the maple cabinets in a U-shape, and a similarly shaped vase was built into the curved maple-and-black-granite kitchen island. Overhead, a curved soffit softens the kitchen's geometry.

The entire first floor opens onto a patio with lake views, while a shared balcony overlooking the lake runs the length of the second-floor bedrooms. Light and airy, the house remains a dream come true for a single mother and her now-adult son.

In the winter, the white house's vertical glass forms glow lantern-like between the front entrance and the lake beyond.

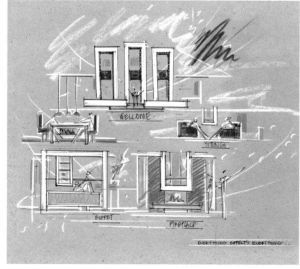

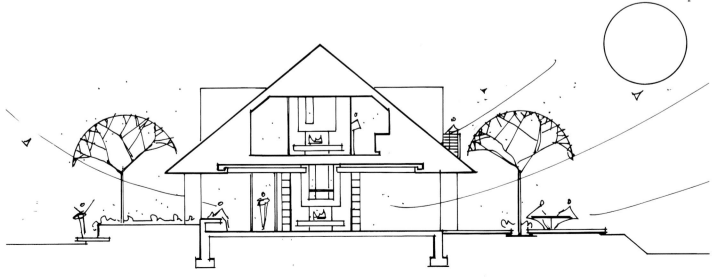

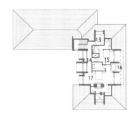

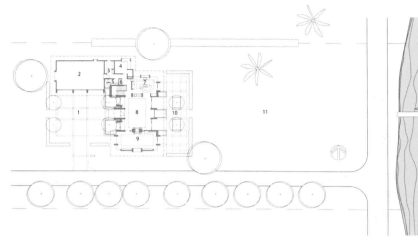

1	Auto court	10	Lake patio
2	Garage	11	Lawn
3	Mud room	12	Dock
4	Study/guest suite	13	Laundry
5	Guest bathroom	14	Gallery/catwalk
6	Pantry	15	Sam's suite
7	Kitchen	16	Lake balcony
8	Great room	17	Leesa's suite
9	Teen room		

The U-shape of the windows proliferates throughout the interior and is found in the mantle of the fireplace, in the kitchen's built-in shelving, and in the shape of an upstairs sleeping space.

A bright color palette of red, yellow, white, and blue is cleanly balanced with glass block and wood accents in the house's open living area, behind which is Sam's media and pool room.

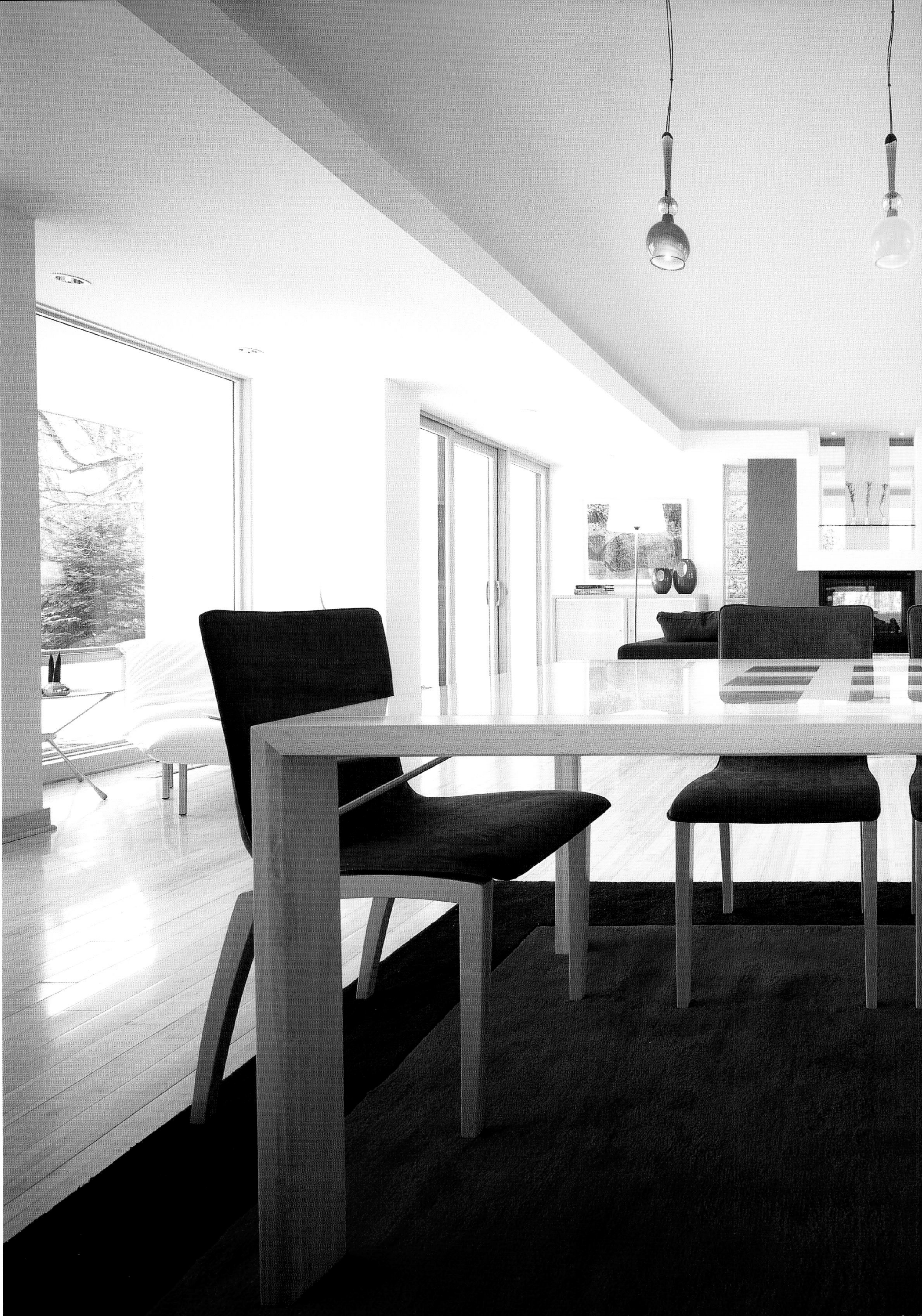

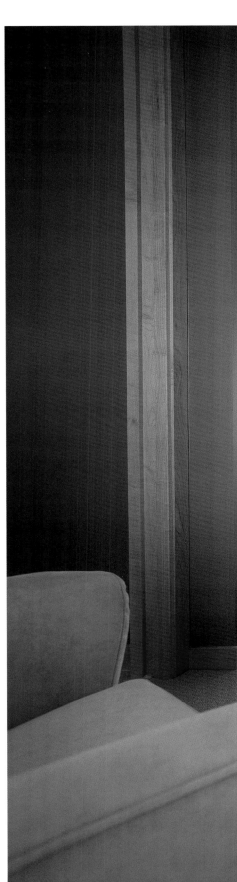

The upstairs hall (opposite top) opens into a master bedroom with lakeside views and fireplace (below). Sam's entertainment area is located on the lower level and shares the fireplace with the living room (opposite bottom).

SEWELL RESIDENCE
Cedar Lake, Minneapolis, Minnesota

Architectural Arabesque

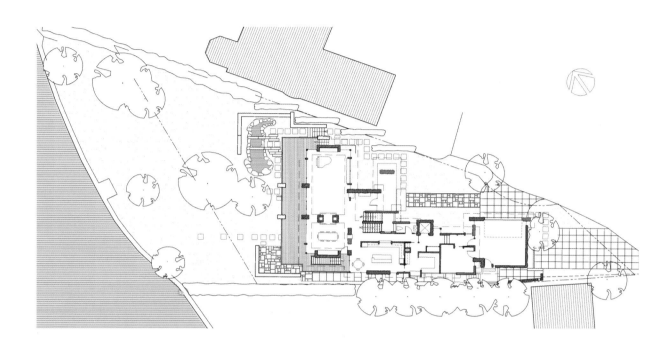

Designed for a family of musicians, dancers, and arts philanthropists, this 5,500-square-foot, three-level home is a harmonic balance of intersecting planes which were as carefully considered as notes on a musical score. To maximize space on the wedge-shaped lot, Stinson initiated the house with a street-side garage and front entrance; then he composed the house to crescendo through the dining area and into a great room with a window wall providing expansive views to Cedar Lake.

In the great room, bands of clerestory windows on the north and east walls admit additional light and focus views into the trees, while rendering adjacent homes invisible. Horizontal soffits add a level of intimacy to the high-walled, airy, light-filled room. Like the ebony and ivory keys on the family's grand piano, black-stained mahogany fins contrast with white walls in the great room; on the house's exterior, black-metal downspouts contrast with pale limestone walls.

A venue for family concerts, the great room has an acoustically tuned maple floor and a limestone fireplace, which also opens to the dining room. Behind the kitchen, which has views into the woods and to Cedar Lake, a stairway leads to the lower level where a media room, wet bar, guest room/exercise room, and practice room open out to the yard. A narrow wall clock, decorated with spiral of tiny maple and blue squares based on architecture's golden mean, is actually a door that opens into the grandchildren's fort beneath the stairs. A glass ledge above the staircase functions as a skylight that brings sun onto a built-in bench in the fort.

Friends invited to concerts at the Sewells' have described the house as a healing, spiritual place. For this growing clan of artists, the house is a home that reflects their values: family, friends, and the arts.

The house is sandwiched into a narrow lot (above) next to a popular urban lake, which the glass-walled living area and front entrance overlook.

Thin white horizontals bisect the limestone columns that define the front entrance (right) and the fireplace area (below).

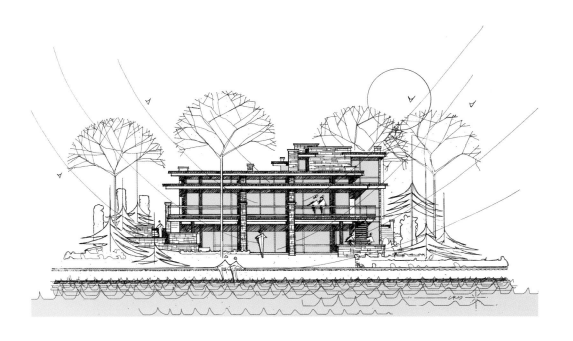

In the kitchen (opposite top), a corner nook of windows overlooks the lake on one end (opposite bottom), while a stairwell with skylight leads to the children's play areas and studios below (left).

On the lower level, the door to the grandchildren's play area has a narrow clock decorated with a spiral of tiny maple and blue squares (opposite top). The lower level opens out to the lake, while the outdoors is also accessed from above via stairways and a balcony (opposite). From the lake, passing canoeists admire the house's stately but simple juxtaposition of horizontal and vertical forms (above).

The residence was built next to an urban lake in Minneapolis, where views of the downtown skyline and wildlife coexist in a natural city setting.

A triangular fireplace of clean-cut cut limestone anchors the open plan of the 5,000-square-foot home, which features a sleek contemporary kitchen of anigre wood and floors of Jerusalem limestone with in-floor heat.

The fireplace was composed within a framework of horizontal and vertical planes to provide shelves for artwork and a window seat (opposite below). Sculpture ledges were also integrated throughout the house (above), including along the stairwell leading to the bedrooms and children's study area downstairs.

BALI RESIDENCE
Wayzata, Minnesota

Stone Temple in the
Woods

After living, working, and collecting art in Asia for a decade, a family decided to return to Minnesota and create a home that would merge their Asian experience with a Prairie School sensibility, as one of the clients had grown up in a Frank Lloyd Wright house. The homeowners asked that the interior be composed of individual rooms, each expressing its own character. And they wanted the house to function not just as a home, but also as a family retreat.

Stinson composed the 8,000-square-foot house to rise organically from its wooded site on columns of oversized, rough-cut, Fond du Lac stone; at the same time, the cedar-shingled hip roof pulls the house back to earth with reverential energy. A stone staircase bisects the structure and its horizontal planes: to the east are stone walls (inspired by a monastery the clients visited) and a cantilevered bench; to the west is a terrace book-ended by fire bowls, with a swimming pool and balé (or open-air pavilion).

Inside the house, Stinson differentiated spaces by varying heights with ceilings, soffits, and clerestory windows, adding stairs that provide transitions from room to room, and using the couple's Asian art, furniture, and artifacts to articulate areas of the house. A teak slab serves as the tabletop in the breakfast booth. Two columns define a hall entrance. A cantilevered bench floats beneath a lighted niche in which a Chinese scroll hangs.

Exposed stone inside and out bring the house into harmony. Fir-framed windows and doors, Venetian-plaster walls, and woods ranging from Brazilian ebony to Minnesota barn siding enhance the house's organic feel. Throughout the house, pin lights on stonework and ceilings add a playful nuance to a comfortable home, which is also a spiritual and family retreat.

The clients' visits to monasteries and temples in Bali influenced the design of the house (above), as well as the creation of an open-air pavilion in which to enjoy the summer months (opposite).

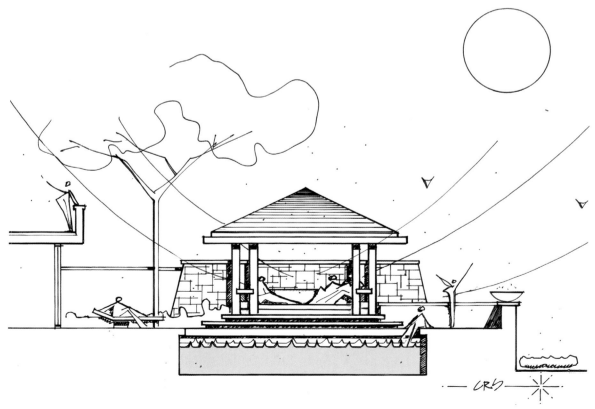

The open-air pavilion at the end of the pool area (above) includes cushions for relaxing or napping in the shade. A balcony and wide stairway offer physical access to the pool area, while cantilevered window wells and ground-level windows walls offer visual access (below).

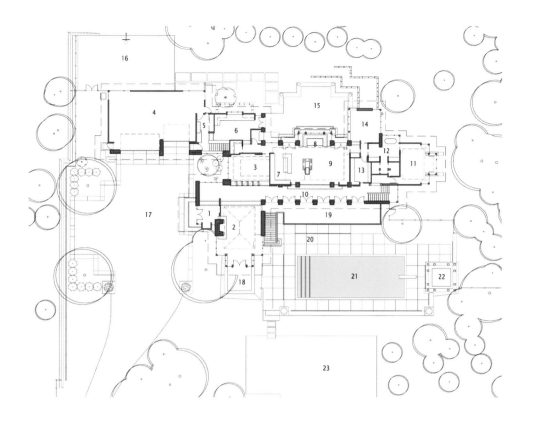

1 Entry
2 Great room
3 Dining room
4 Garage
5 Mud room
6 Laundry
7 Kitchen
8 Breakfast booth
9 Family area
10 Gallery
11 Master bedroom
12 Master bathroom
13 Master closet
14 Study
15 Breakfast terrace
16 Sport court
17 Auto court
18 Great room terrace
19 Gallery terrace
20 Pool terrace
21 Swimming pool
22 Balé
23 Lawn

Light was focused on the perimeter of the interiors, where limestone columns extend from the exterior inside, with broad steps leading up to more enclosed living areas (opposite). One exception is the piano room, with its window walls to the outdoors (above). Artwork was given prominence throughout the house, like this scroll with built-in bench at the entrance (below).

The limestone exterior becomes a rugged earthy accent throughout the house's elegant interior, which includes Venetian-plaster walls, fir-framed doors and windows, and ebony floors.

Designed in part to feature the clients' collection of Asian artwork, the interior includes a teak-slab table in the kitchen (above), and two pillars that denote an entrance to another area of the house (opposite).

LOTUS LAKE NEIGHBORHOOD
Chanhassen, Minnesota

An Architectural Neighborhood
in Tune with Nature

For decades, Ted Delancey followed the career of Charles Stinson, intrigued by the architect's seamless integration of artful architecture within the natural settings of diverse locations. In the 1990s, Delancey approached Stinson with a proposal: would the architect be interested in looking at 9 acres of land, between picturesque Lotus Lake and the town of Chanhassen, as a possible setting for a new, sensitively sited housing development?

The land had been in the Delancey family since 1939. Once a girls' camp operated by Ted's mother, the pristine lakeside setting was filled with mature oak and maple trees, hilly topography, and the evocative foundations of former buildings. Stinson and Delancey agreed to protect the natural features of the area, while also creating an ensemble of houses that together would express one of Stinson's most original architectural compositions.

For several years and through the seasons, Stinson studied the area's sun and shade patterns, views through bare and leafy trees, and road-less geography. As he began planning the site, Stinson's priorities included preserving trees and retaining the land's character. He decided on approximately one house per acre, with a short private drive to each home and only perimeter roads encircling the development.

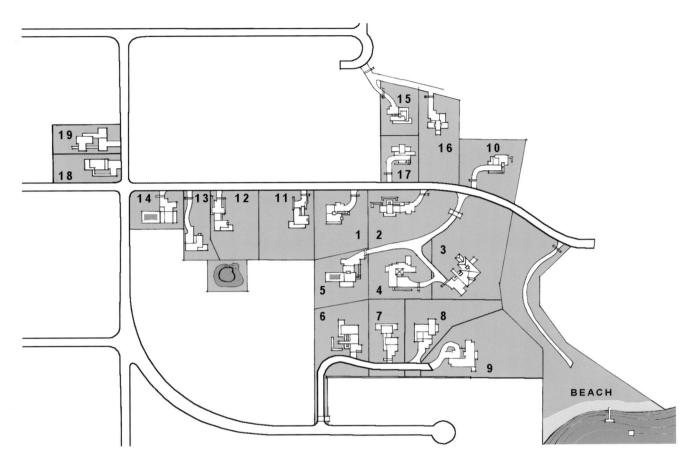

The neighborhood plan includes Stinson-designed homes on wooded lots with only perimeter roads and driveways to help preserve the natural setting.

Each home, created with the lot buyer and future homeowner, is a composition of horizontal and vertical planes that hugs the topography of the site while providing magnificent views of the outdoors from airy light-filled interiors with wide expanses of windows. One of the first structures completed in the Lotus Lake development was a one-story home with lower-level walkout featuring 9-foot ceilings, bamboo floors, built-in maple cabinetry, and leaded-glass doors opening to a cantilevered balcony.

Since then, Stinson has added to the original acreage, and the development now has 19 lots in total.

As Lotus Lake continues to grow, Stinson has maintained his standard of design excellence by creating one house at a time. While each home expresses his signature compositional method, the architecture also honors each client's personality, vision, and lifestyle.

Stinson says, "I've created each house to relate to its site and the particular natural features of that site. So the colors, materials, size, and layout of each home are individual."

In this innovative community, the individual parts create an architectural whole unique to Stinson's oeuvre and planned neighborhoods around the world.

Because this 3,300-square-foot home is tucked into its wooded site overlooking a ravine, Stinson designed a retaining wall, the front entrance, main living areas, and garage to wrap around the auto court in a protective semicircle.

The couple that commissioned this house had relocated from Chicago and desired a contemporary structure with open living and a loft-like feel inside. All of the windows on the main level are sliding-glass doors that open to a deck that extends along the length of the great room/kitchen/dining areas (above, opposite top). The front entry opens into the spacious plan, and a stairway leads to the two bedrooms and office on the walkout level below (opposite bottom).

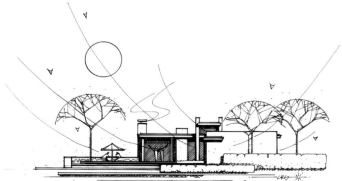

Commissioned by a musician and her husband, this home features a front entry framed with two slender doors and articulated floor-to-ceiling windows that transparently connect with similar doors and windows on the opposite side, and open to the woods, creating a glass jewel box for the piano and adjacent listening area.

Ted and Kathy Delancey's 4,200-square-foot house, the first in the development, includes a large screen porch with a vaulted cedar ceiling (opposite), and a 20-foot-long deck that extends into the trees to provide a variety of spaces for outdoor living on the site (above).

148

A modern glass box in the woods, this 4,500-square-foot home was designed with a gallery-like entry foyer for the display of art (opposite left), and features industrial materials such as a simple wood stair rail supported on metal pegs (opposite left) and a steel fireplace (opposite right). The four-bedroom home has a pyramid roof of standing-seam metal that provides a vaulted ceiling space inside to bring light into the gallery and the open-plan living spaces (above).

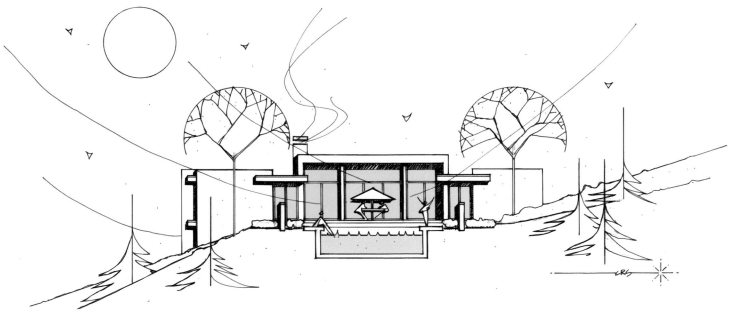

This client asked for a modern, 3,000-square-foot house with a pool in the new development. For maximum privacy, the pool is framed on either side by stucco walls, and the 12-foot-high window wall in the open living space opens directly onto the pool, as do the master suite and guest bedrooms/office on either side.

152

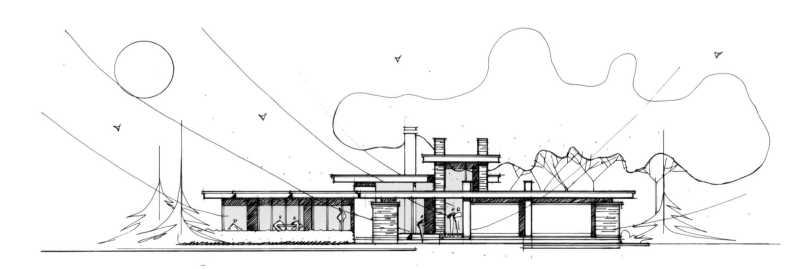

The 5,000-square-foot house for a retired couple is a composition of
broad verticals in white stucco and brick, and slender horizontals
outlined in dark red and white fascia.

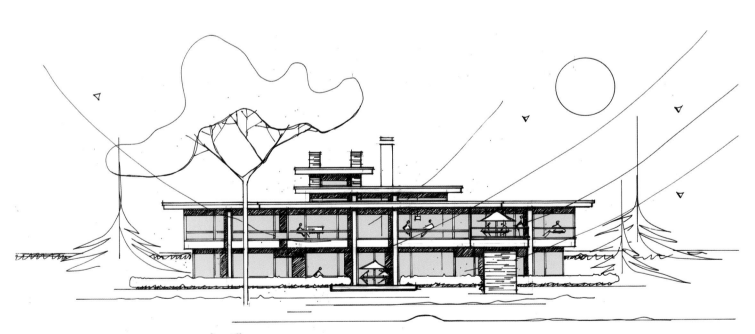

The brick forms continue inside where they support walls of wood-framed windows and a fireplace with a white flat surface for displaying art (left). Doors, trim, and floors throughout the house are a variegated red maple (opposite top). The kitchen is a simple square form with red Silestone counters, upper cabinets of glass, and lower cabinets of lacquered white for an eclectic aesthetic (above).

The entry foyer, bracketed by 16-foot-high brick columns, is reached through a covered area alongside the garage (below), or from a stone walkway connecting the house with its grassy site (left).

158

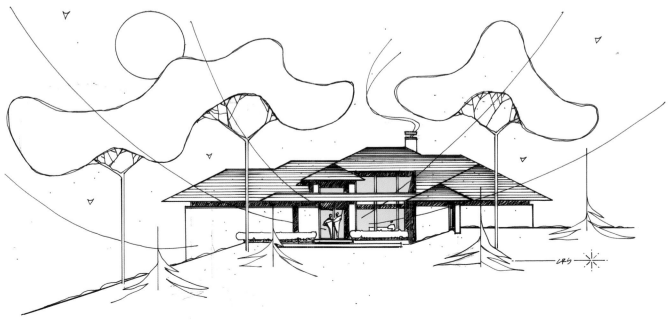

This unobtrusive 4,000-square-foot house in a muted color palette was nestled into the woods and provides views into the trees from large windows in the great room, which features a high ceiling with skylights carved out from the hipped roof.

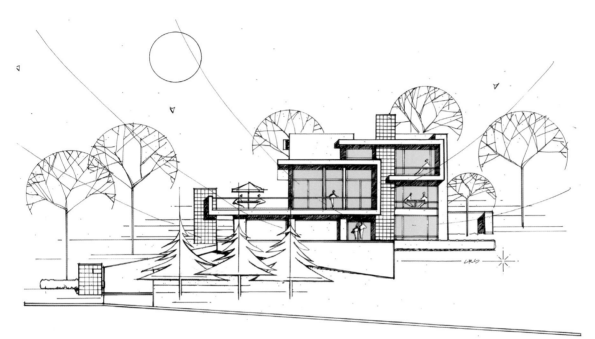

Lot #10 has become one of the development's signature homes. Composed on a steep hillside to allow for broad views of the trees and nearby lake, the three-level home is composed of statuesque rectangles that gradually recede into the woods as they rise up on the site. An artful addition to Stinson's architectural composition is the rough-hewn concrete block wall, which repeats as a vertical sculptural element on either side of the house, most notably as an interior/exterior wall that becomes a chimney-like support as it rises through the house.

From the ground level—with its European-style auto court and woodland-facing guest bedrooms— the house flows to a main level with open great room, living area, and kitchen opening to a balcony. The homeowners elected not to include a fireplace, as from the start the design brought in enough ambient natural light from the outdoors to warm the house. An open stairway connects all three levels and leads to what Stinson calls "the crow's nest;" a master suite 50 feet above ground with expansive views of the natural setting.

One of the development's signatures, this 3,200-square-foot home was sited on a steep hillside for expansive views through windows and from balconies of the trees and nearby lake.

The colorful interior features varying ceiling heights to define areas such as the intimate dining room (below), and the spacious living area (opposite). Large wall expanses serve as gallery space for displaying the homeowner's art collection (right).

162

An open staircase connects all three levels of the home (opposite), and leads to a master suite 50 feet above ground with views of the natural setting (below).

The loft-inspired stairway also defines areas within the open-plan main level (above), which opens onto a balcony and expansive outdoor living area (opposite).

NORTH AMERICAN FINANCIAL CENTER
Willmar, Minnesota

Bank Statement

For almost 20 years Brian Borgerding had enjoyed his Stinson-designed home. So when the CEO of North American Financial Center needed to oversee the design and construction of a new banking facility, he challenged Stinson to compose a light-filled, welcoming financial center that would serve as a community gathering place.

The 23,000-square-foot building's strong horizontal planes move from the stucco exterior inside to the building's atrium as clerestory windows, soffits, and a second-floor terrace that serves as an employee lounge. The horizontals join at a 40-foot-tall fireplace in the center of the atrium, which anchors the structure and symbolizes the bank's strength, longevity, and role as a community financial hearth.

The building's blue-tinted low-e windows are framed with Douglas fir to enhance the building's residential feel. Stinson also specified Douglas fir for floors, millwork, information desks, and teller stations. Tan-and-gold ceramic tile

complements the limestone and custom concrete block of the walls and fireplace. The entire structure is heated and cooled by geothermal wells underneath the parking lot.

In addition to a bank, the building houses a community room, a coffee shop with outdoor courtyard, an insurance agency, a real-estate office, and the office of a financial planner. The North American Financial Center is a destination for the community's financial needs, housed in an architectural sculpture on the prairie.

Strong vertical and horizontal forms firmly hold broad swaths of glass in place, conveying both permanence and transparency in the bank building.

The subtle patterning of the custom-concrete block on the bank's exterior (left) continues inside on the walls and fireplace, which ground the spacious interior (below).

The fireplace and adjacent vertical forms anchor the floating horizontals and open-railing balconies that rise up through the bank's interior (above and opposite).

Clerestory windows ensure continuous daylight throughout the interior while reinforcing the long lines of the soffits and balconies (opposite top and below). Within the juxtaposition of forms, Stinson created enclosed spaces for meetings and conferences (below).

Douglas fir millwork frames glass walls and doorways, while
built-in cabinetry adds smoothness and warmth to the tactile
ridges of the block walls (above and opposite).

COLE'S SALON & SPA
Apple Valley, Minnesota

One of the firm's residential clients asked the office to bring a sense of intimacy and comfort to this commercial project, which was accomplished with warm stone in the entry, and curved forms and soffits that define areas and lower ceiling heights.

The salon area replicates a forest, with wrapped-wood columns branching off into individual wood-paneled stations and circular-soffited lights forming a canopy overhead.

GOOD SHEPHERD LUTHERAN CHURCH
Green Bay, Wisconsin

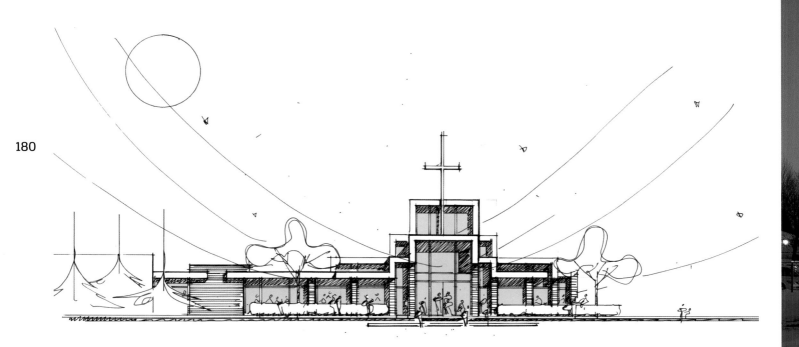

Steve Schoen, a builder with whom the firm works, brought this project to the the office. Long horizontal expanses of glass framed in white stucco on the front side (above) symmetrically step up to the sky in the middle, creating a sanctuary bracketed with glass that draws light high and deep into the building (opposite).

CAMPBELL SUNROOM
Madison, Wisconsin

Sunroom Addition

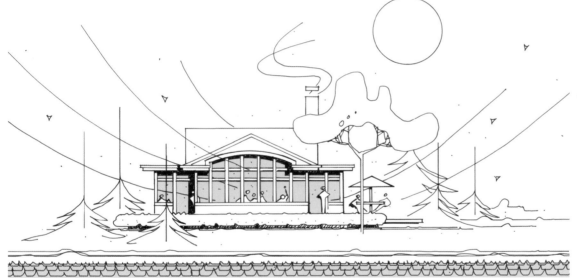

The homeowner (Stinson's sister) desired a four-season porch at the back of her existing house, with operable casement windows to let in the summer breeze. From inside the house, French doors open into the spacious sunroom with curved cherry-wood ceiling and vertical windows topped by arches.

BILTMORE ON CEDAR LAKE
St. Louis Park, Minnesota

Urban Viewfinder

On this three-lot development tucked beside a picturesque city lake, Stinson completed his first loft-like home that marries a modernist aesthetic with an urban natural environment. A solid base of limestone block, custom cut with a tile-like finish, anchors the 4,000-square-foot house's main level, which cantilevers toward the lake with views of the outdoors through window walls or from a broad terrace protected by roof overhangs.

The black vertical window framing is juxtaposed with the composition's white horizontal forms to create dynamic feelings of stability and release. Two structural cross-walls of limestone, one of which also forms the chimney, bisect the floor planes and introduce the stone to the interior. In addition to the massive fireplace, the limestone tile reoccurs inside on selected walls and floors.

The house's interior composition pivots around a central steel-framed stairwell, with oak treads and steel-cable rails, which rises 22 feet. The living areas, as well as private bedrooms, open through glass doors to east- or west-facing patios, ensuring an easy transition between indoors and outdoors. Venetian-plaster walls and white-oak flooring throughout the house enhance its uncluttered composition.

The project's other two houses, currently in design development, will combine with the first to create a single architectural composition in which a modern, downtown aesthetic complements wildlife watching at an uptown lake.

In the low-profile house, the first in the Biltmore development, large expanses of picture windows punctuate the sturdy massing (opposite).

Long window bands bring light through the walls while protecting the homeowners' privacy, and lead the eye to the window wall overlooking the lake at one end (left).

A textural concrete fireplace, wood floors, and glass expanses create a materiality
throughout the house that's at once rugged and elegant.

The house's patterned concrete base topped with broad bands of seamless white stucco protects the inhabitants from the noise and traffic of an adjacent roadway.

KIRVIDA RESIDENCE
North Lindstrom Lake, Minnesota

Emerging from the sloped site to take advantage of lake views, the
house's stucco walls are topped with copper fascia, while stone pillars
support a deck that extends the length of the house.

To bring warmth and intimacy to the 5,500-square-foot home, the ceilings were clad in wood throughout the first level. The stair rail to bedrooms on the lower level was constructed of wood ribbons connected with glass (above). Smooth, horizontal cedar ceilings and soffits merge with rough limestone columns in the living areas, creating nooks for reading, a fireplace, and artwork (above and opposite).

A variety of open living spaces are tied together with fir-framed clerestory windows, cedar ceilings, and maple cabinetry (opposite). In the kitchen, the anigre-wood ceiling merges with clean-lined cabinetry (opposite).

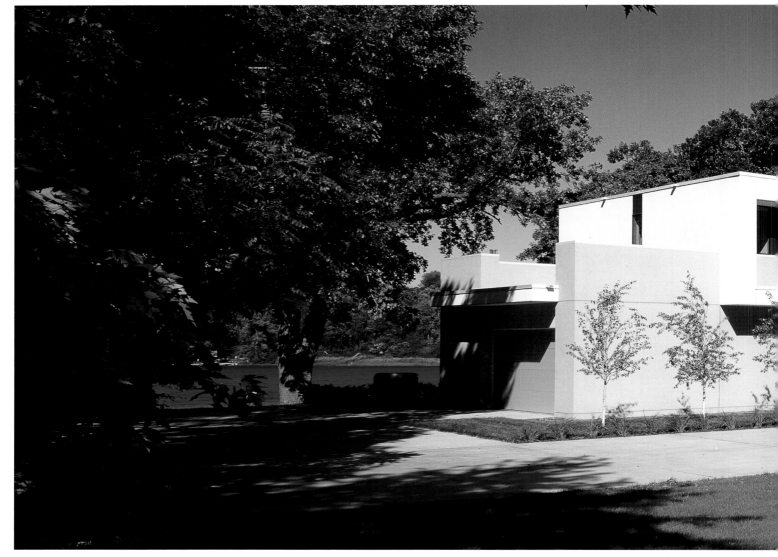

From the street side, the residence maintains a private stance with strong vertical and long horizontal forms shielding windows (above). On the lake side, the ratio of glass to stucco forms is reversed, so that thin horizontals frame wide expanses of glass overlooking the lake.

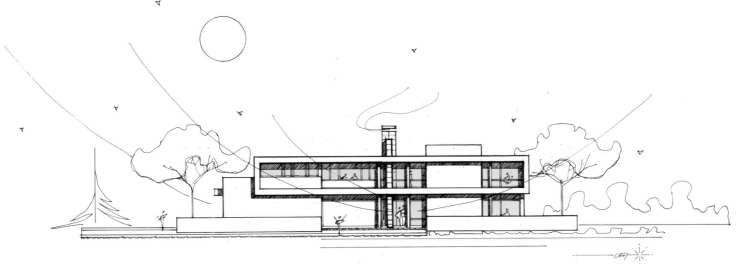

SIEGEL RESIDENCE
Excelsior, Minnesota

Treetop Modernism

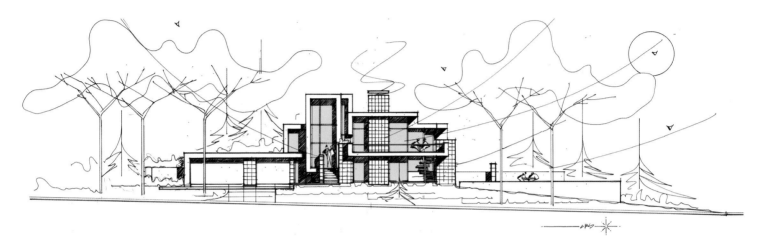

Designed as a northern summer retreat for a retired couple, the house has since become their year-around home because of its sleek aesthetic, light-filled living spaces, and panoramic views of the lake and woods. To provide those views and capture light, Stinson "floated" the main level of the 3,300-square-foot residence—a simple composition of white horizontals and window ribbons, which are bisected by grey chimneys and black window framing—on top of a glass box. Inside the lower-level box are a guest suite, sauna, media room, study, and an artist's studio.

Nestled into the trees, the upper main floor features an open great room with a window wall on the lake side and transom windows opposite. A concrete-block fireplace accentuates the room's tree-top-high ceilings. The great room is also open to a modern kitchen warmed with maple accents and a cozy breakfast nook. A slim snackbar/island separates the kitchen from the dining area. A master bed and bath, and a guest suite (which also serves as a yoga room) are also located on the main level.

To enhance the house's treetop modernism Stinson designed a 12-foot-tall, charcoal-colored form, which is planted with small trees, along the exterior of the great room. A wrap-around terrace provides the homeowners with unobstructed views of trees and woods, whatever the season.

Tall black-framed glass windows, recessed in white stucco juxtaposed with thin charcoal-colored forms, mark the house's entrance.

The house steps lightly across its site via an ensemble of floating geometric forms bound together with white vertical and horizontal framing (previous pages).

The front door opens into a cool, white, high-ceilinged entry, with stairways and inner balconies outlined in a warm wood railing (above and opposite).

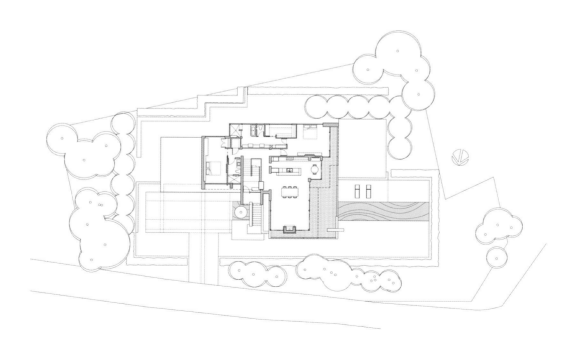

The kitchen, dining and living areas flow easily together, with a low band of windows providing light and views while shielding the inhabitants from passersby (opposite). The more enclosed cooking and eating area opens into casual living space with floor-to-ceiling glass windows opening onto balconies and offering views of the woods (above and below).

An open, modern feel permeates the interiors, whether upstairs from the front entry in the formal gathering area (opposite), the spacious bath (top), or a hallway leading to the outdoors (above).

Sited in a woods filled with wildlife, the house provides the homeowners with multiple possibilities for outdoor living, including balconies, patios, and walls of windows with views to the outdoors.

LAKE HARRIET HOME
Minneapolis, Minnesota

Urban Lakeside Loft

A young, artistic family moving back to the city asked Stinson to compose a home full of light and energy from which they could incorporate the bustle of a public urban lake or retreat into a private dwelling. They also requested an industrial, loft-like aesthetic of steel and glass, along with warm woods, natural light, and expansive views.

The complex program was fulfilled with a dynamic 5,000-square-foot composition of horizontal and vertical lines (differentiated by white or grey stucco) that steps up on its site to allow light into every room while maintaining the homeowners' privacy. The lines defining the exterior of the house also extend through the structure's interior, generating an open living/kitchen/dining area in which clerestory windows atop horizontal soffits, and floor-to-ceiling windows juxtaposed with vertical columns, allow in bountiful light and views of the lake without leaving the occupants on display.

Exposed fir was used to construct the built-in window seats, the front-entry closet, the paneled ceiling in the three-season porch, and the kitchen cabinetry. In contrast, a staircase of

stretched airplane cable and steel, ribbed-glass cigarette windows on the stair's upper landing, and museum-style reveals between walls and baseboards give the house its industrial feel.

Upstairs, the parents' bedroom suite, with built-in storage and terrace, overlooks the front yard and nearby lake. On the north end, the daughter's bedroom suite includes a reading room with built-in shelves, a terrace with rain drains in the same bubble pattern used in the glass block of the laundry,

and a secret fort with windows overlooking the auto court.

On the ground, a stacked bluestone wall hides the circular auto court (which doubles as a bicycle racetrack) from public view. To the south, the house sits on a curved bluestone staircase that steps down to a sunken lawn. In his composition of seeming opposites—cool and warm, private and public, visible and invisible—Stinson created the ideal urban lakeside home for a family to live and work, rest and play.

Located next to a busy urban lake and parkway, the house is settled into its lot with a protective wall curving around the front and enclosed play area in the back.

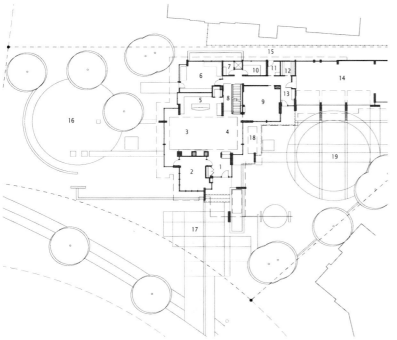

1   Entry
2   Three-season porch
3   Great room
4   Dining area
5   Kitchen
6   Study
7   Powder room
8   Stair tower
9   Studio
10 Laundry
11 Dog room
12 Closet
13 Mud room
14 Garage/workshop
15 Dog run
16 Lawn
17 Guest court
18 Trellis
19 Auto/play court

216

The house casts a warm glow when lit from within during the evenings; but the curving walls (opposite top) and the positioning of windows, soffits, and built-ins give the inhabitants privacy from peering eyes along the parkway (above and opposite).

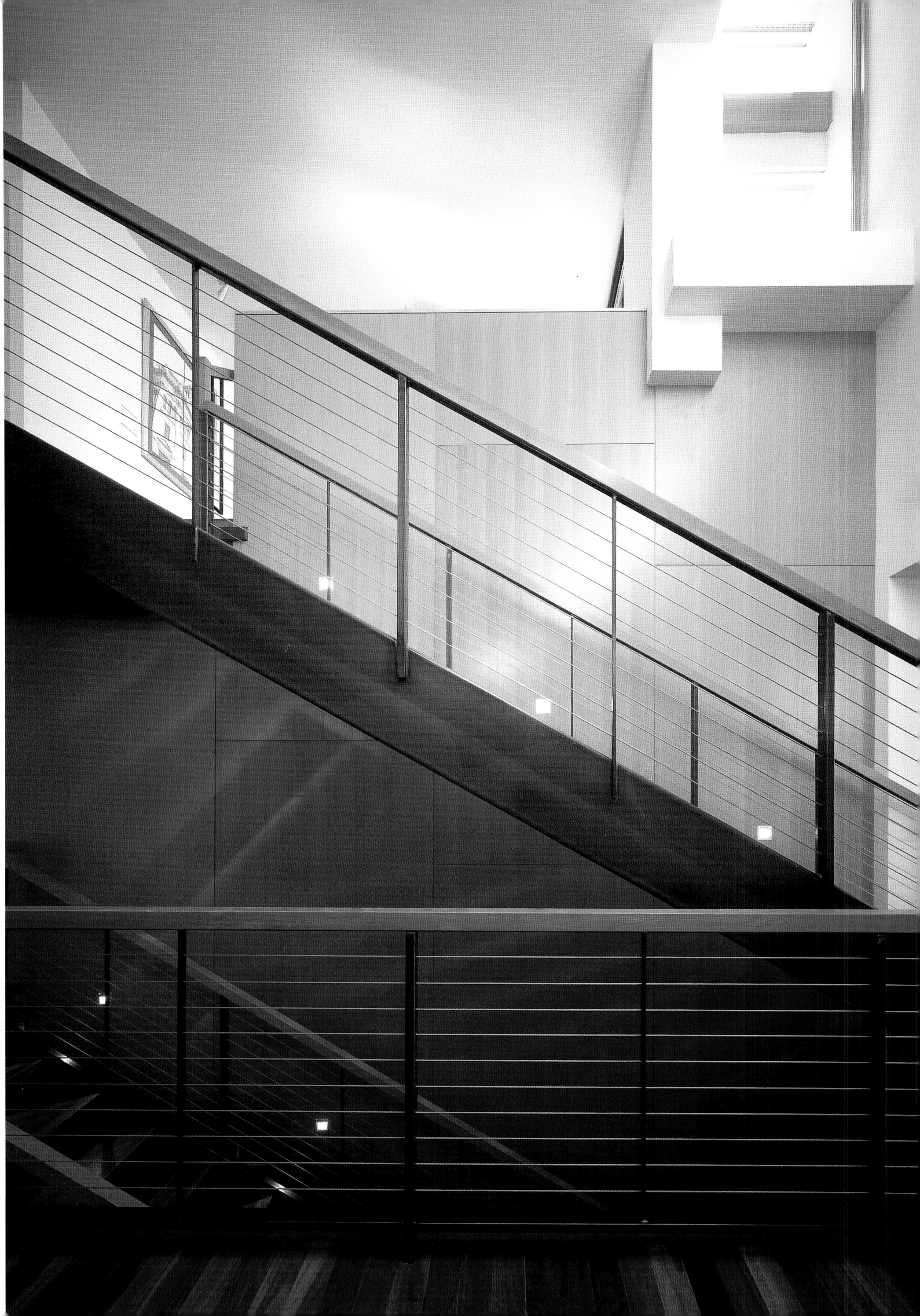

Airplane cable along the stairwell helps give the interior the industrial, loft-like feel the homeowners asked for (opposite). The living areas range from colorfully furnished open spaces that flow into the kitchen and dining areas (above) to more nook-like reading and relaxing areas in which wood ceiling panels and vertical supports give the room a human scale (left).

Slices of the outdoors are available even through narrow openings visible along the stairwell (opposite), which leads to children's library and reading area with windows overlooking the backyard (above) and the parents' master bath (below).

A curved, stacked-limestone wall gives the backyard auto court privacy on the street side (above), while white stucco walls open to the auto court and garage from the alley (opposite).

ON THE DRAWING BOARD

CRUTCHFIELD RESIDENCE
Hidden Creek
Mendota Heights, Minnesota

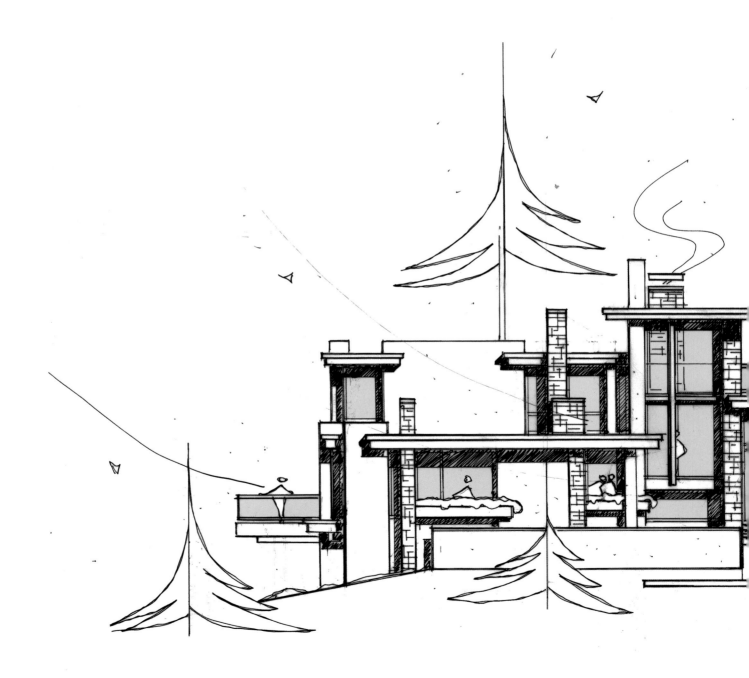

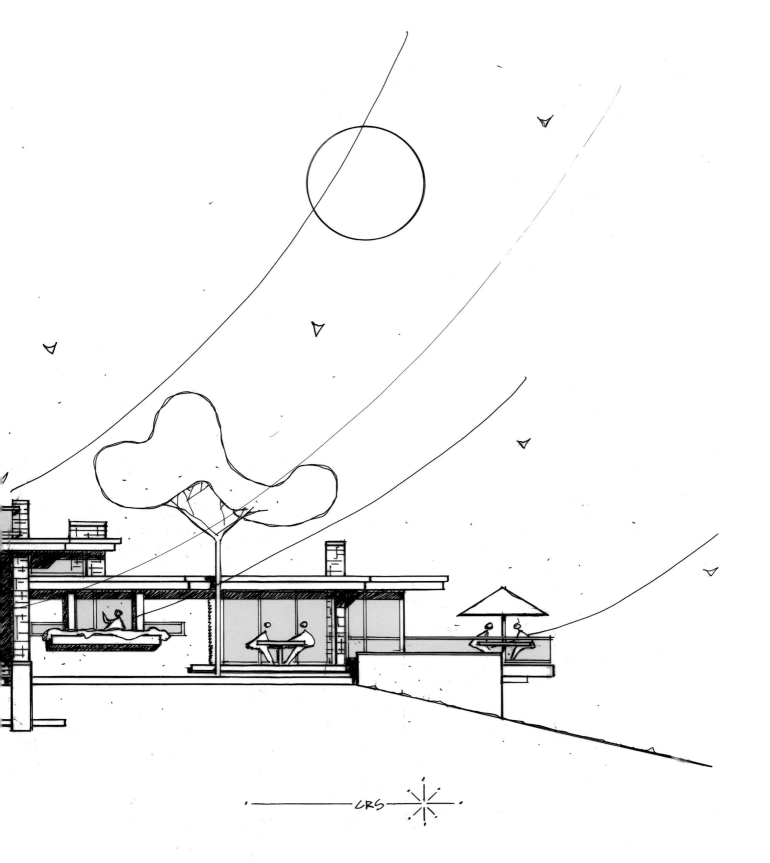

CRS

LOT #19 LOTUS LAKE
Joshua Stinson, Farmhouse Renovation
Chanhassen, Minnesota

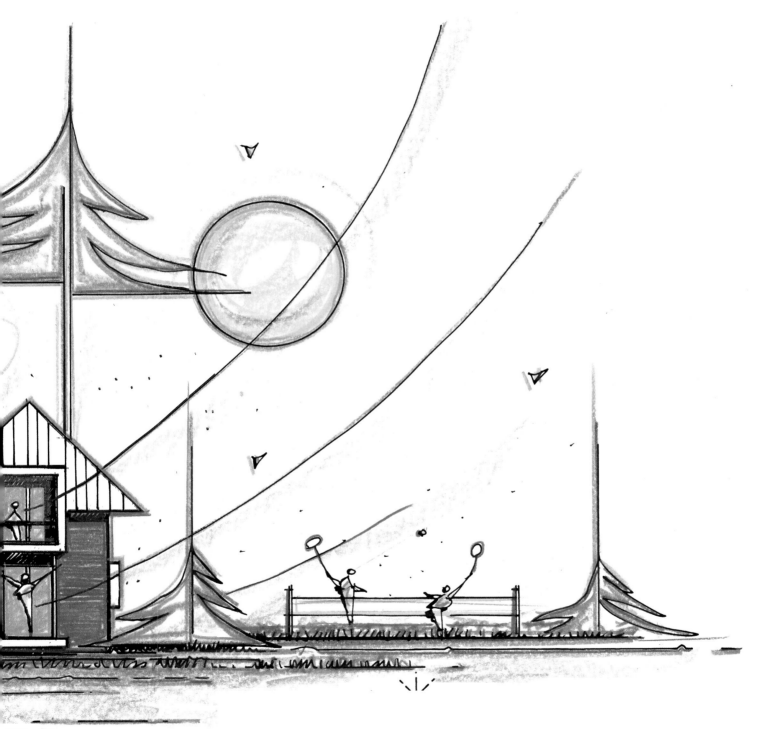

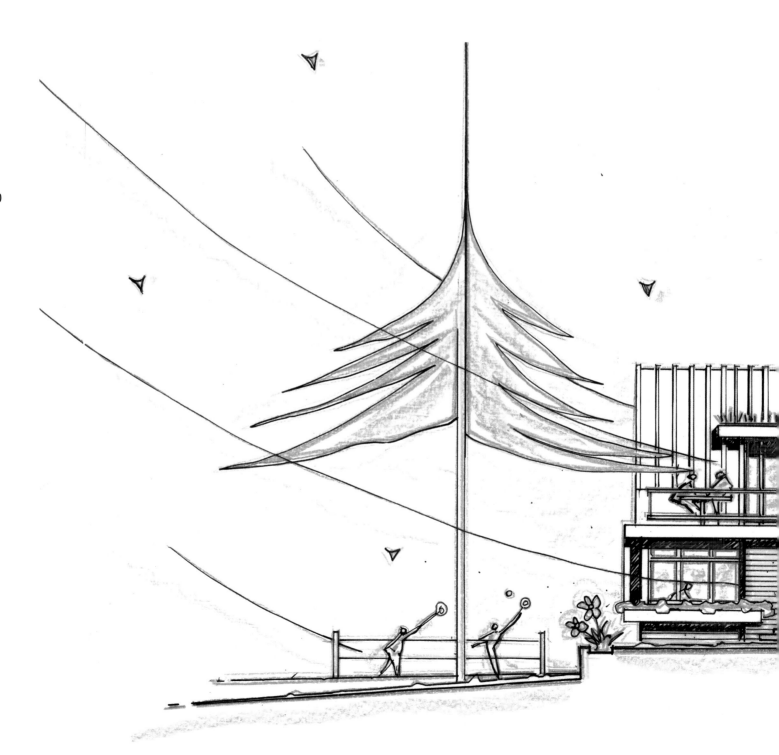

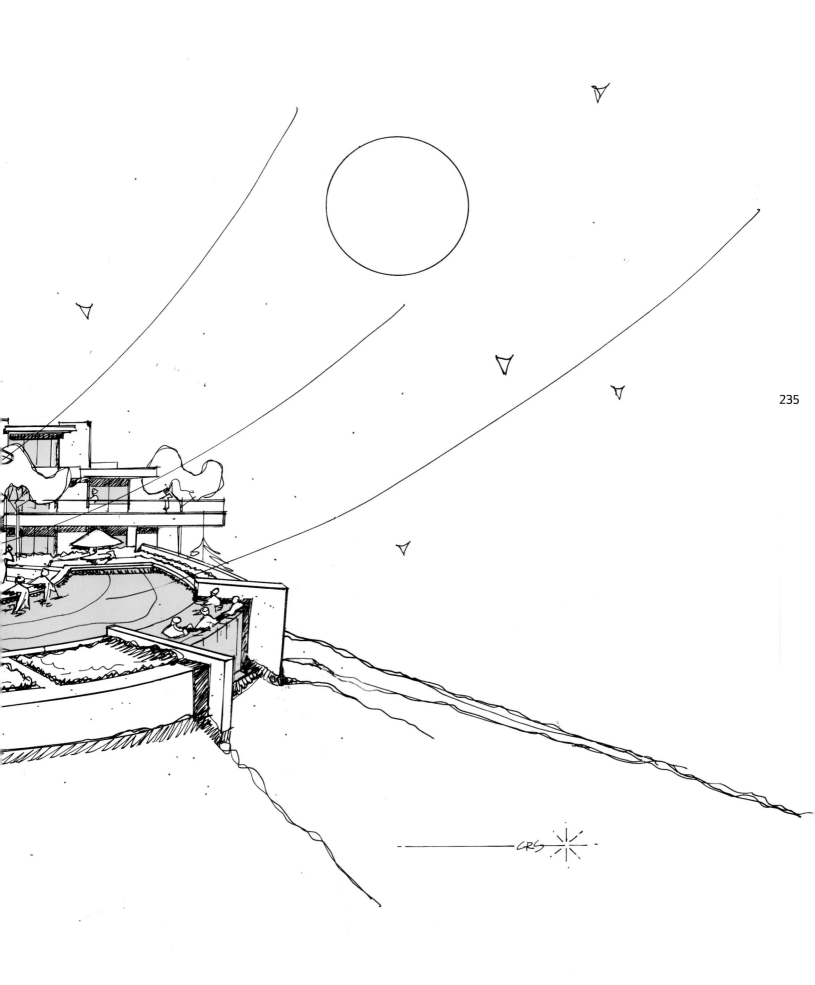

MONTE BELLO
Playa Hermosa, Costa Rica

LAKE CALHOUN RESIDENCE
Minneapolis, Minnesota

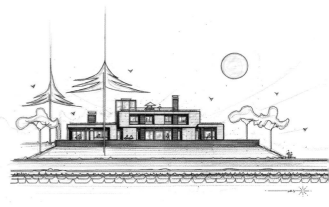

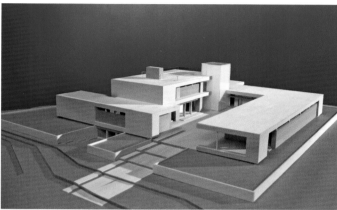

240

242

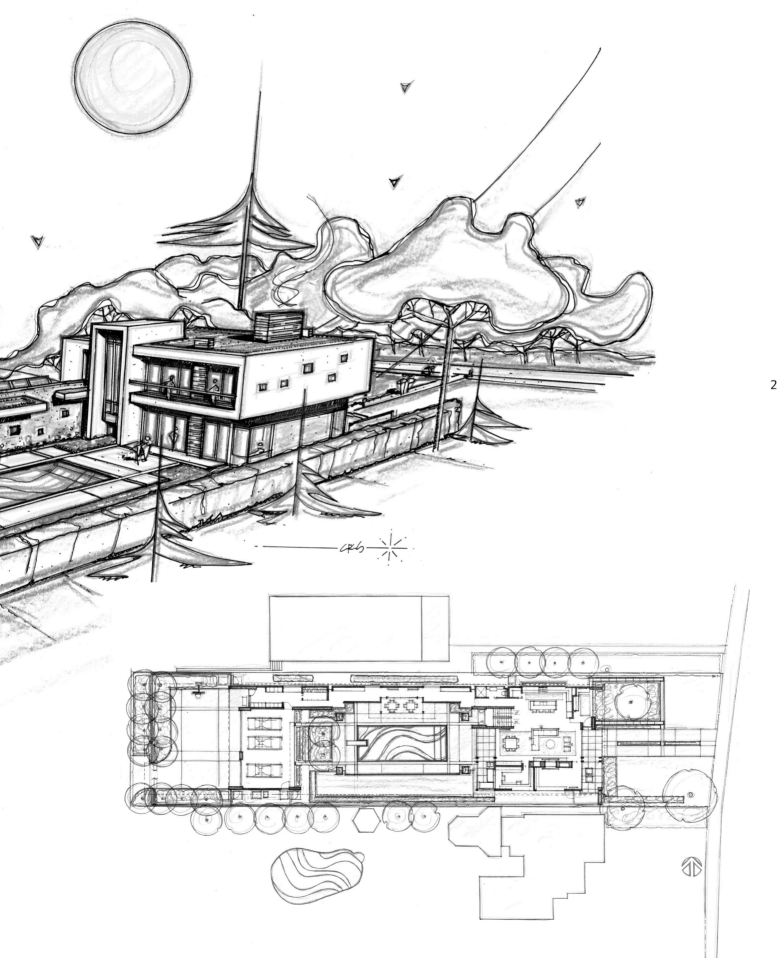

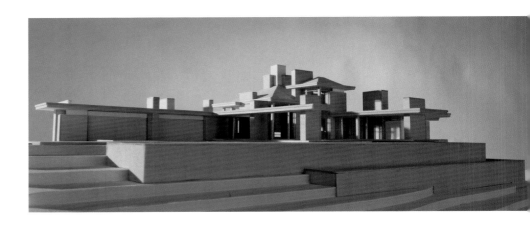

246

APPENDIX

CRS

Standing, left to right: Douglas Fletcher, Larry Ward, Chuck Thiss, Charles R. Stinson, Larry Glenn, Ruth Johnson

Seated, left to right: Tess Riabokin, Bill Potter, Nicole Norris, Carol Eastlund, Robin Edstrom

ACKNOWLEDGMENTS

There are many to whom I owe gratitude and thanks for the existence of this book. The journey unfolded over years, but it began with you, my clients, and your eagerness to realize a vision. You provided amazing opportunities to explore, create, and collaborate. And to these you added the gift of friendship—even the moment we first met, I felt as though I'd known you for years. Thank you for entrusting me with your dreams. It has been a great ride!

To Peter Balstinelli-Kerze, without your images there would be no book. You have made me a better architect. Through the honesty of your photography I have learned to see more truthfully, to appreciate beauty more profoundly. When you work you step into another world, and bring back in pictures the dance of light and space as if we are actually there to experience it. The images in this book span an evolution of architecture, as well as an evolution of a working relationship into a deep friendship. Thank you.

Streeter & Associates built nearly all of the completed buildings in this book. Together, we have seen more than one hundred projects realized—what an accomplishment! The quality of your workmanship and professionalism has raised the bar for the entire industry. Thanks to all of you: Steven, Donald, Kevin, Justin, and the whole Streeter team.

Camille, you have always understood our work and how to translate it into words. Your writing skillfully takes readers from the grand concepts to the fine details. You are a master. You get us. Thank you for helping this book become a reality.

To my professional heroes, I humbly and gratefully bask in the light of your teachings: architect, James Stageberg; architect and Dean of the School of Architecture at the University of Minnesota, Ralph Rapson; architect, Frank Lloyd Wright; and artist, Charles Biederman. You have fed and guided my inspiration from the earliest days. It is through you that this work has emerged.

A special thanks to the following individuals for helping to make this book possible: Kristen Clay, Chuck Thiss, Douglas Fletcher, Tess Riabokin, Barbara Dunlay, Janell Siegfried, and Robyn Beaver.

The final and dearest thanks belongs to my "family of creators," the people with whom I have the privilege to work every day. When I walk into our studio my spirit soars—the environment we've grown for ourselves is a dream come true. Each of you contributes to the greater whole with unfailing passion, enthusiasm and commitment to the collaborative process. And, therein we find our reward: to freely, joyfully co-create. I can't think of anything better than that. My heartfelt thanks to you all: Chuck, Bill, Larry G., Douglas, Larry W., Ruth, Nicole, Tess, and Robin.

PROJECT CREDITS

Altman Residence
Interior: Faye Gallus
Builder: Streeter & Associates
Landscape Architect: Damon Farber & Associates
Cabinets: Scott Terwilliger, Sunray Metal Roofing: Aldo, Inc.
Structural Engineer: Mike Preston, MJP Structural Engineering Consultants

Bali Residence
Interior: Owners
Builder: Streeter & Associates
Landscape Architect: Todd Irvine, Keenan & Sveiven
Cabinets: Scott Terwilliger, Sunray
Stone: Mike Nelson, Nelson Concrete
Structural Engineer: John Retka

Bealeu Residence
Interior: J.K. Interiors
Builder: Streeter & Associates
Landscape Architect: Jim Hanson Landscaping
Cabinets: Scott Terwilliger, Sunray

Biltmore on Cedar Lake
Builder: Streeter & Associates
Landscape Architect: Coen + Partners
Kitchen: Valcucine
Stone: Mike Nelson, Nelson Concrete
Structural Engineer: John Retka

Burt Residence
Interior: Owners
Builder: Roy Burt; Kevin Streeter Consulting
Landscape Architect: Jim Hanson Landscaping

Campbell Sunroom
Interior: Ann Campbell
Project Manager: Charlie Campbell

Carlson Residence
Interior: Gary Hovda
Builder: Streeter & Associates
Cabinets: Scott Terwilliger, Sunray
Structural Engineer: John Retka

Charles R. Stinson Architects & CRS Interiors
Interior: CRS Interiors
Builder, Phase I: Streeter & Associates
Builder, Phase II: Jason Stinson, Stinson Builders, Inc.
Landscape Architect: Scott Frampton, Landscape Renovations
Green Consultant: Joshua Stinson

Cole Residence
Interior: J.K. Interiors
Builder: Streeter & Associates
Landscape Architect: Coen + Partners
Cabinets: Scott Terwilliger, Sunray
Stone: Mike Nelson, Nelson Concrete
Structural Engineer: Mike Preston, MJP Structural Engineering Consultants

Cole's Salon & Spa
Joint Venture Architects: Charles R. Stinson Architects with Alan Plutowski of AJP Architects
Interior: CRS Interiors
Builder: Pete Pulk
Salon and Spa Manager: Jennifer Wilson

Corson Residence
Interior: Gary Hovda
Builder: Streeter & Associates
Landscape Architect: Damon Farber & Associates
Cabinets: Scott Terwilliger, Sunray
Structural Engineer: Mike Preston, MJP Structural Engineering Consultants

Fleming Residence
Interior: Gary Hovda
Builder: Streeter & Associates
Cabinets: Scott Terwilliger, Sunray
Structural Engineer: John Retka

Gempeler Penthouse
Interior: CRS Interiors

Good Shepherd Lutheran Church
Interior: CRS Interiors
Builder: Steve Schoen, Schoen Construction
Landscape Architect: Charles R. Stinson Architects

Kirvida Residence
Interior: CRS Interiors
Builder: Streeter & Associates
Landscape Architect: Charles R. Stinson Architects & Landscape Renovations
Structural Engineer: WR Design

Kurowski Residence
Interior: Ann Kurowski
Builder: Streeter & Associates
Landscape Architect: Scott Frampton, Landscape Renovations
Structural Engineer: Heyer Engineering

Lake Harriet Home
Interior: Clients with CRS Interiors
Builder: Streeter & Associates
Landscape Architect: Damon Farber & Associates
Cabinets: Scott Terwilliger, Sunray
Structural Engineer: Mike Preston, MJP Structural Engineering Consultants

Leesa and Sam's House
Interior: CRS Interiors with Ligne Roset
Builder: Streeter & Associates
Landscape Architect: Charles R. Stinson
Cabinets: Brad Braaten, Braaten Creative Woods
Structural Engineer: John Retka

Lotus Lake Neighborhood
Lot #1
Interior: CRS Interiors with Ligne Roset
Builder: Streeter & Associates
Landscape Architect: Charles R. Stinson Architects & Landscape Renovations
Cabinets: Brad Braaten, Braaten Creative Woods
Structural Engineer: Mike Preston, MJP Structural Engineering Consultants

Lot #2
Interior: Marlene Burrell
Builder: Streeter & Associates
Landscape Architect: Damon Farber & Associates
Structural Engineer: Mike Preston, MJP Structural Engineering Consultants

Lot #3
Interior: J.K. Interiors
Builder: Streeter & Associates
Cabinets: Scott Terwilliger, Sunray
Structural Engineer: John Retka

Lot #4
Interior: Faye Gallus
Builder: Streeter & Associates
Landscape Architect: Damon Farber & Associates
Cabinets: Scott Terwilliger, Sunray
Structural Engineer: Mike Preston, MJP Structural Engineering Consultants

Lot #5
Interior: Kay Touchette
Builder: Streeter & Associates
Landscape Architect: Scott Frampton, Landscape Renovations
Structural Engineer: John Retka

Lot #7
Interior: CRS Interiors
Builder: Streeter & Associates
Landscape Architect: Coen + Partners
Cabinets: Brad Braaten, Braaten Creative Woods
Structural Engineer: WR Design

Lot #9
Interior: Ligne Roset
Builder: Streeter & Associates
Structural Engineer: John Retka

Lot #10
Interior: CRS Interiors
Builder: Streeter & Associates
Landscape Architect: Charles R. Stinson Architects & Landscape Renovations
Kitchen: Valcucine
Stone: Mike Nelson, Nelson Concrete
Structural Engineer: Mike Preston, MJP Structural Engineering Consultants

Nordahl Residence
Interior: J.K. Interiors
Builder: Streeter & Associates
Cabinets: Scott Terwilliger, Sunray

North American Financial Center
Joint Venture Architects: Charles R. Stinson Architects with HTG Architects
Interior: CRS Interiors & Jayne Vetter
Builder: Breitbach Construction Company
Landscape Architect: Coen + Partners
Structural Engineer: McConkey Johnson Soltermann, Inc.

Private Residence, Olympic Hills, Minnesota
Builder: Streeter & Associates
Cabinets: Scott Terwilliger, Sunray
Structural Engineer: Mike Preston, MJP Structural Engineering Consultants

Private Residence, Rolling Green, Minnesota
Interior: Gary Hovda
Builder: Gary Alick
Landscape Architect: Damon Farber & Associates

Rohan Residence
Interior: J.K. Interiors with Ligne Roset
Builder: Streeter & Associates
Structural Engineer: John Retka

Ron Dittmar Marina Village
Project Manager/Builder: Ron Dittmar

Sewell Residence
Interior: Tom Gunkleman
Builder: Streeter & Associates
Landscape Architect: Damon Farber & Associates
Cabinets: Scott Terwilliger, Sunray
Stone: Mike Nelson, Nelson Concrete
Structural Engineer: Mike Preston, MJP Structural Engineering Consultants

Siegel Residence
Interior: CRS Interiors
Builder: Streeter & Associates
Landscape Architect: Coen + Partners with Landscape Renovations
Cabinets: Brad Braaten, Braaten Creative Woods
Stone: Mike Nelson, Nelson Concrete
Structural Engineer: Mike Preston, MJP Structural Engineering Consultants

Stinson/Eastlund Residence
Builder Phase I: Streeter & Associates
Builder Phase II: Jason Stinson, Stinson Builders, Inc.
Landscape Architect: Charles R. Stinson Architects with Scott Frampton
Green Consultant: Joshua Stinson
Structural Engineer: Mike Preston, MJP Structural Engineering Consultants

Streeter/Wettengel Residence
Interior: Gary Hovda
Builder: Streeter & Associates
Landscape Architect: Jim Hanson Landscape
Cabinets: Scott Twilliger, Sunray
Structural Engineer: Mike Preston, MJP Structural Engineering Consultants

Wilson Residence
Interior: Charles R. Stinson Architects
Builder: L. Cramer Co.
Structural Engineer: Mike Preston, MJP Structural Engineering Consultants

Zawistowski Residence
Builder: Kyle Hunt & Associates
Structural Engineer: John Retka

On the Drawing Board

Crutchfield Residence
Builder: Streeter & Associates
Interior: Laurie Plattes Interiors
Landscape Architect: Todd Irvine, Keenan & Sveiven

Lot #19 Lotus Lake, Joshua Stinson
Farmhouse Renovation
Co-designer: Joshua Stinson
Builder: Jason Stinson, Stinson Builders, Inc.
Project Manager/Co-builder: Joshua Stinson
Interior: CRS Interiors
Green Consultant: Joshua Stinson

Stinson/Hedlund Residence
Builder: Jason Stinson, Stinson Builders, Inc.
Interior: CRS Interiors

Pollei Residence
Builder: Jepson West & John Bloomster
Interior: CRS Interiors

Yath Residence
Builder: Streeter & Associates
Interior: CRS Interiors
Landscape Architect: Todd Irvine, Keenan & Sveiven

Pacific Ocean Residence
Builder: Tom Terry, Grupo ConstrucTom S.A
Interior: CRS Interiors

Lake Calhoun Residence
Builder: Streeter & Associates
Interior: CRS Interiors and Coen + Partners

Minarovic Residence
Interior: CRS Interiors

Naujokas Residence
Interior: Debra Naujokas

Stinson/Larson Residence
Builder: Jason Stinson, Stinson Builders, Inc.
Interior: CRS Interiors
Green Consultant: Joshua Stinson

Ivie Residence
Interior: CRS Interiors

BIBLIOGRAPHY

Altman Residence

Kudalis, Eric. "Residential Geometry." *Architecture Minnesota*, May/June 2008, 44–47.

Bali Residence

LeFevre, Camille. "Resting Spot." *Architecture Minnesota*, May/June 2006, 44–45.

"Home for all Seasons." *Home & Apartment Trends*, Volume 21, Number 6, 8–17.

"Rustic Ambiance." *BathroomTrends*, Volume 20, Number 9, 58–59.

"Nature's Embrace." *BathroomTrends*, Volume 20, Number 9, 136–139.

"Home for all Seasons." *Home & Architectural Trends*, Volume 21, Number 1, 62–71.

Robyn Beaver (Ed). *100 More of the World's Best Houses,* The Images Publishing Group: Melbourne, Australia, 2005.

Biltmore on Cedar Lake

Walsh, Jim. "Lofty Idyll." *Midwest Home*, August 2006, 152–155.

"Urban Alternatives." *Home & Architectural Trends*, Volume 22, Number 6, 110–128.

Charles R. Stinson Architects & CRS Interiors

LeFevre, Camille. "Orchestrating Space" and "Architect of Distinction" award. *Midwest Home & Garden,* March 2005, 38–43.

Lake Harriet Home

LeFevre, Camille. "Elegant Geometry." *Architecture Minnesota,* May/June 2005, 52–56.

O'Connor, Joe. "Nod to Modernism." *Twin Cities Furnishings,* Volume 9, issue 2, 2001, 40–43.

"Natural Affiliation." *Home & Architectural Trends,* Volume 22, Number 6, 8–19.

Beaver, Robyn (Ed). *100 More of the World's Best Houses.* The Images Publishing Group: Melbourne, Australia, 2005.

"All under one roof", *Home & Architectural Trends*, Volume 26, Number 6, 9–19.

Leesa & Sam's House

Yun, Sejan. "Extraordinary Contemporary." *Twin Cities Furnishings,* Volume 5, issue 2, 2001, 16–20, 31.

"Nahki Residence." *Yapi,* February 2005, 44–47.

LeFevre, Camille. "Color Play." *Architecture Minnesota,* May/June 2003, 38–42.

Beaver, Robyn (Ed). *A Pocketful of Houses,* The Images Publishing Group: Melbourne, Australia, 2006.

Beaver, Robyn (Ed). *Another 100 of the World's Best Houses,* The Images Publishing Group: Melbourne, Australia, 2004.

Lotus Lake Neighborhood Lot #10

Baltus, Michelle. "Light Box." *Midwest Home & Garden,* August 2005, 140–145.

Steiner, Andy. "Light and Air." *Twin Cities Spaces,* Spring/Summer 2007, 42–47.

Steiner, Andy. "Light and Lines." *Twin Cities Spaces,* April/May 2007, 48–55.

Private Residence, Lake Minnetonka

Shea, Kitty. "Quintessence." *Midwest Home & Design,* Fall 2005, 64–67, 78.

Rohan Residence

Crooke, Carolyn. "Belle Vue De Lac." *Twin Cities Furnishings,* Volume 6, issue 6, 2002, 18–23.

Ron Dittmar Marina Village

Kudalis, Eric. "CoastalWaves." *Architecture Minnesota,* November/December 1998, 36–37.

Sanders Residence

Suttell, Robin. "Natural Instincts." *Beautiful New Homes,* Winter 2001, 76–79.

Sewell Residence

LeFevre, Camille. "Architectural Aria." *Architecture Minnesota,* May/June 2002, 40–45.

Beaver, Robyn (Ed). *Another 100 of the World's Best Houses,* The Images Publishing Group: Melbourne, Australia, 2004.

"Concert Piece." *Home & Architectural Trends,* Volume 18, Number 6, 12–21.

Greve, Kristie. "Living Sculpture." *Midwest Home & Garden,* February/March 2002, 38–45.

Siegel Residence

Robyn Beaver (Ed). *The New 100 Houses x 100 Architects,* The Images Publishing Group: Melbourne, Australia, 2007.

Ford, Alyssa. "Lighthouse on the Lake." *Midwest Home & Garden,* March 2008.

Stinson/Eastlund Residence

LeFevre, Camille. "Playing Pool." *Midwest Home,* May 2007, 58–61.

Knox, Barbara. "Reaching for the Light." Mpls St. Paul magazine, September 1994, 94–97, 109.

256